Goal Crusher

The Ultimate Guide to Achieve Big Audacious Goals

April Smith

Goal Crusher, The Ultimate Guide to Achieve
Big Audacious Goals

Written by April Smith

Copyright © 2023
Daily Execution Planner, LLC

ISBN: 979-8-218-33138-2

Dedication

For my parents, Janice and Douglas Smith.

Thank you for your sacrifices. Thank you for giving me the best childhood and feeling of home that I could ever desire. I love you so much!

To my big sister Janell for being an example and my first friend.

To my besties, for encouraging and supporting me through every goal and triumph:
Sherry Trotter, Lamond Hull, and Terra Washington.

This book would not have been possible if I hadn't exposed myself to new environments and invested in myself. In 2020, my perspective on life changed, and I committed to personal development like never before. Along the journey, I met Alowe McCants and Remiah Trask who empowered me to write this book. Being an author was nothing I imagined for myself, but they guided me through the process and gave me the confidence to believe it was possible. Thank you for being my amazing coaches!

Table of Contents

Introduction

Are you existing or living? Is your life filled with daily commitments of work and errands? Do you find yourself in moments of boredom that lead to falling into the abyss of "Netflix and Chill" or falling asleep to the reruns of your favorite childhood TV show?

In the midst of our busy, mundane routines and constant competing priorities that take our attention, are settled whispers tempting us to chase fleeting ambitions. It's not until life happens that we start thinking about living again. When there is a death of a loved one, we realize how short life is, and we start to reflect on our own lives. Or we get inspired by someone else's dreams coming true, and we say to ourselves, "Oh, good for her!" or "One day, I'm going to open my own salon," or "Someday, I will start a charter school." And then, we do nothing... it's just a thought.

Well, I decided to write this book because I want to help you go after your deep desires, dreams, and aspirations. I'm all about less talk and more action. My friends and family jokingly said, "Man, April, you are so discreet and secretive about what you do." Well, my intention is not always to announce what I'm doing. I simply just do it. What is there to talk about? I let my work speak for itself.

Think about it: when women are first pregnant, they are advised to wait for 12 weeks before announcing it because the chances of a miscarriage are much higher within the first 12 weeks than at any other point in the rest of the pregnancy.

This is the same philosophy with a goal. There's a higher rate of you giving up on a goal within the first 12 weeks. You may or may not take action if you don't have a plan; you could fail. And here you are, shouting to the masses about what you are going to do before you have done any real work to birth the idea or goal. It's the most risky point because everyone you talk to will have an opinion about your goal, and they will try to tell you what is or is not possible because they have never done it. No one cares what your friends think.

God gave you the vision. He didn't schedule a conference call with you and all your friends to discuss it – He called YOU.

It surprises me how many people either do nothing with their goals or tell everyone what they are going to do but don't do anything. Then, I realized that not everyone's brain is wired the same way.

I learned through a personal self-assessment test that I am a "Pilot." The pilot tends to think big picture and does not waste time with irrelevant facts or small talk. Pilots want results NOW and have a need to be in the driver's seat. Pilots are usually described as Driven, Decisive, Determined, Aggressive, Specific, and to the point. We are very task-driven people who execute at a high level, and we're all about the work, less about the talk, simply getting things done! And only 12% of the population actually has this trait.

Executing comes very naturally to me, which explains why I gravitated to my profession as a Project Manager. As a project manager, I create plans and organize people to execute tasks. Every day, I help Fortune 100 and 500 companies execute strategies and objectives set by their corporate officers. The principles that I use to help companies are the same principles I use to achieve my goals, no matter how big or small.

For example, I said I wanted to go to Greece to experience Santorini, Mykonos, and Crete. And I did it. I wanted to experience the peace and serenity of Bali. I did it! I wanted to see what the big deal was about Dubai. And, an opportunity presented itself, so I went! I wanted to take a trip alone, so I went to Morocco with a group of complete strangers. Done! I hit these goals in less than two years!

I did the same thing for my career when I decided that I wanted to be a project manager. I became a Project Management Professional and got my PMP certification to legitimize my expertise. Once I had that certification, I took it a step further and pursued my MBA, not just any MBA, but an MBA from a top 20 business school. I had multiple trials and tribulations to get there, but I stayed focused on the goal, and I graduated from Emory-Goizueta Business School. Done! I realized over time that as I started to hit my goals, my visions and desires became bigger and bolder.

Over time, my mindset started to shift because my exposure expanded, and my hunger for more intensified. The more I was exposed, the bigger and bolder my goals and my ability to execute became even more efficient.

In 2022, I realized I had perfected the concept of setting and executing goals. Every 90 days, I was hitting a goal. In the first quarter of 2022, I flipped and sold a single-family property out of state. In the second quarter of 2022, I invested in one of my favorite restaurants in Atlanta.

Then, in the third quarter of 2022, I purchased a 4-unit property in Chicago that I house-hacked. In the last quarter of the same year, I launched the "One Day" brand and released a 90-Day Daily Execution Planner. I hit all these goals while juggling a demanding 9-to-5 position at a Big 4 consulting firm.

I am at a point where I have discovered my goal-setting approach is effective, and it really works for me. Now, I want to share the frameworks that I use to help you achieve your big audacious goals.

In those quiet moments of wishful thinking stands the quiet power of purposeful goal-setting. Purpose is not just an abstract term; it's your internal compass that guides your decisions and fuels your ambition. It permits us to start living and experiencing all there is to experience in this amazing world. You can start living the life you want by simply setting a goal and making your one-day, someday goal a reality by taking it one day at a time. Just think about it for a minute, you can completely change your life by simply setting a goal. Not just any goal, but a big audacious goal.

Over time, the concept of setting goals has changed. Gone are the days of setting basic 'New Year's Resolutions' that fade by February. We have entered an era where goals are more than just checkboxes; they are the stepping stones to our desired life.

Goals transform us when they are bound to a more profound sense of purpose. They become alive, driving us forward even when the initial enthusiasm dies. With purpose, goals are not burdens; they are gateways to fulfillment. They inspire us to become the best versions of ourselves and live the life we desire.

I welcome you to read this book and let it transform your life and inspire you to go after your big audacious goals by taking it one day at a time. It is really up to you if you want to go after your goals; if not, you can close the book now. But if you are looking to do something different and go beyond what you do every single day with the same mundane life experiences, keep reading this book. And join me on this journey to help you evolve, be, do, and have the things you want and become the ultimate Goal Crusher.

What to Expect from This Book

Let me help you start living again. This is not an invitation, but a call to action, to redefine and to go after goals that give you purpose and permission to live the life you desire.

In this book, I will dive into the distinction between ordinary goals and Big Audacious Goals (BAGs). Understand what separates them and why striving for the latter can be life-transforming.

You will learn the systematic approach to creating your ideal life. From the initial visualization to actionable steps, I will guide you through a process to ensure your goals are aligned with your deepest desires.

You will be equipped with powerful mental tools, from understanding the benefits of gratitude to harnessing the energy of affirmations and "I am" statements. These are your armory against doubts, challenges, and potential setbacks.

Time is a limited resource, and in this book, I will give you actionable time-management strategies tailored for goal-crushing. Discover the art of crafting routines that suit your lifestyle and propel you closer to your dreams, one day at a time.

Understand why celebrating milestones, no matter how small, can be your secret weapon in maintaining momentum. Plus, gain insights into the power of reflection in ensuring consistent growth.

Then, apart from wisdom and strategies, this book comes with prompts to reflect and templates to put the concepts into action. They are designed to provide you with tangible steps for your goal-setting journey, making the process not just theoretical but deeply practical.

As you turn each page, you are not just reading; you are taking charge, transforming, and gearing up to conquer every challenge, every dream, every goal. The time to unleash your ultimate potential is now. Are you ready to crush your goals?

Let's begin.

Chapter 1:

Understanding Goals

Throughout our lives, we often clutch our dreams and aspirations as tightly as a cherished love letter from a high school sweetheart. But holding on without taking action is merely preserving a wish. Remember Langston Hughes' poignant question: "What happens to a dream deferred? Does it dry up like a raisin in the sun?" In this chapter, I aim to illuminate the true essence of a goal. We'll delve deeper to unravel the nuances of a Big Audacious Goal (BAG) and pinpoint the fundamental differences between standard goals and BAGs.

Let's start with a goal:

A goal is a clearly defined objective or target an individual aims to achieve within a specific period. It serves as a direction or focus towards which efforts and actions are directed.

I am sure you understand the basic definition of a goal. This definition isn't anything brand new or earth-shattering, but what if you REALLY understood the intended purpose of a goal? I mean, really understood it? A goal is meant to propel you from where you are to where you are destined to be. They serve as catalysts. They are the building blocks that drive progress, foster growth, and define success.

One of my mentors, Damon Dillard, shifted my perspective on goals. He suggested looking at the word 'goal' as an acronym: G= Go, O=Out, A=And, L=Live. He explained that you cannot live the life you desire if you stay within the basic and traditional definition of a goal. He broke GOALS down into 3 Levels:

Level 1: Safe Goals

These are the goals well within your wheelhouse—objectives you've accomplished before and can reasonably expect to achieve again. Think of basic but necessary achievements like losing 10 pounds, paying off debt, or increasing your income. They are your bread-and-butter aspirations!

Level 2: Stretch Goals

These are goals designed for growth, pushing you just beyond the boundaries of your current capabilities. They require some level of sacrifice, whether it's moving to a brand-new city or taking a significant risk that genuinely challenges you. Stretch goals might make you second-guess yourself, but they encourage you to stretch beyond your comfort zone.

Level 3: Supernatural Goals

These are your audacious, beyond-the-realm-of-immediate-possibility goals. They're so ambitious that you might not even know the steps to reach them, yet you can visualize them with crystal-clear clarity. Often, they can't be easily explained by logic or the laws of nature. If vocalizing these goals makes you hesitate, fearing people might think you're delusional, then you're on the right track! These are the dreams that redefine what you consider possible.

Forget ordinary aspirations like Safe Goals and Stretch Goals; aim for the transformative power of Big Audacious Goals (BAGs) instead. We're not talking about designer handbags; we're referring to life-altering B.A.G.s—goals so monumental they'll demand a seismic shift in your belief system.

These aren't just goals; they are revelations that will compel you to evolve so that you and those around you will observe a profound transformation. You'll grow into them, and as a result, you will experience a profound paradigm shift that alters your perspective on what is possible.

These BAGs exist beyond conventional wisdom and the natural laws that govern our lives. They propel you into uncharted territory, pushing you to accomplish feats no one in your circle has ever achieved. Prepare to step far beyond your comfort zone, shedding outdated beliefs.

These audacious goals will challenge you to dismantle and reevaluate everything you thought you knew, shattering your limitations and expanding your sense of what's possible. These goals will make you go to God with bold requests, and God will use your testimony as an example of what He can do. You just have to take action and go after them.

Let's stay on this concept of BAG just a tad bit longer. Let me break down the key characteristics of Big Audacious Goals (BAGs) because I really want you to grasp this concept; if you don't get this, you will completely miss the point of this book.

Key Characteristics of BAGs are:

Scale: Monumental, often spanning years or even decades. They challenge the status quo and reshape landscapes.

Inspiration: BAGs are designed to inspire not just the individual setting them but wider communities and societies.

Long-Term Vision: Unlike goals, BAGs envision a distant future, a radical transformation that alters trajectories.

Challenge: BAGs are inherently difficult, demanding innovation, perseverance, and tenacity.

I think you've got it! Now let's make this practical so you can really reflect on this.

1. **What are some of the safe goals that you have achieved in the last five years?**

_____
_____
_____
_____
_____
_____
_____
_____
_____
_____
_____
_____
_____
_____
_____
_____
_____
_____
_____
_____
_____
_____

2. What are some of the stretch goals that you have achieved in the last five years?

_____
_____
_____
_____
_____
_____
_____
_____
_____
_____
_____
_____
_____
_____
_____
_____
_____
_____
_____
_____

3. What are some of the big audacious goals you have achieved in the last five years?

_____
_____
_____
_____
_____
_____
_____
_____

_____
_____
_____
_____
_____
_____
_____
_____

Now tally up how many goals you have achieved for each category:

Safe Goals:_____

Stretch Goals:_____

Big Audacious Goals:_____

What if we could reverse the count and go after more Big Audacious Goals and Less Safe Goals in the next 90 days? Would you be interested? Turn the page, and let's find out how.

Chapter 2

The Ideal Life Framework

To establish big, audacious goals, it's essential to start with life visioning—a process dedicated to identifying your "Ideal Life."

The quote, "If you give them permission to feed you, then you give them permission to starve you," struck a profound chord when I first encountered it in 2020, amid the pandemic's onset. Millions were jobless, and remote work became a universal mandate. The realization unnerved me: my fate was essentially in the hands of a corporate entity, which could eliminate my position at any time. Was I prepared for such a contingency?

In the midst of global uncertainty, I chose to shift my focus from uncontrollable external events to my thought process. My mind was awash with an endless stream of news updates, articles, and varied opinions on the nature of "essential workers," and it was draining me emotionally and mentally. I felt a strong need to distance myself from this barrage of information.

So, I orchestrated my own "Silent Retreat" within the sanctuary of my living room. After informing my family and close friends of my 24-hour disconnect, I eliminated all distractions—no television, no internet, and absolutely no conversation. It was a comfortable solitary confinement with my thoughts and God, hours of meditation.

While meditation is a regular practice that grounds me, this experience was transformative. It drastically altered my mindset, perspective, and, ultimately, my life's trajectory.

I made a solemn vow to myself: I would not be the same individual emerging from the pandemic as the one who had entered it. I aspired for evolution and greater fulfillment; life's brevity demanded nothing less. This led me to pose a crucial question: What is my Ideal Life? And thus, my journey in life visioning began.

The initial step in life visioning involves entering a meditative state to pose deeply reflective questions with sincerity:

What is trying to emerge in my life?

What is my gift to share?

What is my purpose?

Why am I here?

What is attempting to unfold?

These inquiries should be asked with the understanding that the answers will resonate uniquely with each individual, as they are predicated upon one's personal relationship with spirituality. Being attuned to subtle signs and intuitive guidance is vital, as these answers will inform your vision of your "Ideal Life."

Your Ideal Life encompasses various facets—well-being, relationships, career, business, family, finances, and personal growth. It is the sum of the daily experiences that bring you joy and satisfaction.

The notion of an "Ideal Life" is inherently subjective, varying according to individual values, aspirations, and life situations. Take time to ponder deeply: What does your Ideal Life look like? What do you truly desire?

It sounds cliché to say, "The world is your oyster," but it's so true! Everything you wish for is attainable. Rekindle your child-like imagination to visualize your goals and mentally play them out. But the first step is defining your desires; the challenge is in the execution. Don't worry, stick with me through this book, and I'll guide you on how to execute – that's not the intent of this chapter. We will get to it later.

The mechanics of reaching your ideal life are secondary; the paramount consideration is knowing precisely what you desire.

As time unfolds, whether it's in mere minutes, days, or even months, you'll receive your answers. These will manifest through subtle whispers, intuitive flashes, minor signs, gentle nudges, symbolic representations, and newly inspired dreams. Each hint serves as a directive from a higher power, guiding you toward realizing your ambitions. Whether it's a sudden urge to make a particular phone call, to venture out for a walk, or to initiate a conversation with a stranger at a coffee shop, these subtle actions are the stepping stones leading you to what you've declared you want. It's the divine answering your questions and charting your course.

Patience is essential here, coupled with a readiness to tune in. As you listen attentively and make yourself available to these divine cues, you'll begin to make incremental progress in the right direction. These small steps, seemingly inconsequential in isolation, cumulatively build inertia, which eventually transforms into momentum. As this occurs, doors will open, opportunities will unveil themselves, and your life vision will evolve into a guiding force.

The goals that emerge from this exercise will serve as the roadmap for your journey toward your ideal life, providing a foundation for the realization of your most audacious aspirations. I promise you this visioning process sets the stage for everything that follows.

Let's transform these visions into tangible reality by elevating the exercise a notch higher. Dedicate a quiet afternoon to create a vision board. A vision board is two-dimensional; it's a visual of your ideal life and acts as a source of inspiration. To truly manifest your dreams, it's crucial to both see and emotionally engage with them.

Step 1: Set the mood by playing your favorite music and indulging in your preferred snacks or beverages.

Step 2: Think about the images and objects that resonate with your concept of an ideal life.

Step 3: Gather these images either from print magazines or through online platforms like Google Images.

Step 4: With scissors and glue at hand, create a collage that represents your aspirations, weaving in inspirational words and phrases. Enjoy the process as you map out your desires.

Step 5: Place your completed vision board in a location where you will regularly see it, ensuring your aspirations remain at the forefront of your consciousness.

For a more immersive experience, let's venture beyond the vision board and physically interact with our dreams in the real world—a three-dimensional exercise that engages all five senses.

The objective is to familiarize yourself with the environments and experiences that align with your goals. Immerse yourself in the surroundings you aspire to inhabit: the homes, the cars, the communities, and the relationships. The idea is to condition both your mind and body to believe you genuinely belong in these spaces. Unless you become comfortable in these envisioned settings — despite potentially not having had the privilege to frequent them—you're unlikely to attain them. You won't acquire what you don't believe you deserve.

The adage "act like you've been here before" is applicable. Familiarize yourself with these dream environments so that when you do arrive, it feels like a homecoming rather than foreign territory.

Over time, as you continually orient your thoughts towards these aspirational realities, your life will naturally start to resonate with them. The environments that most frequently occupy your thoughts are the ones you're likely to manifest. If you don't actively disrupt this pattern, you risk remaining stagnant, acquiring skills but never truly transitioning into your ideal life settings.

So, pause for a moment to jot down the experiences you wish to have in your ideal life. List them comprehensively below.

Consider the steps you can take immediately or in the near future to experience a taste of your vision. Is there a particular neighborhood you should explore? A specific hotel where you might spend a night? An upscale restaurant you wish to dine at? Could you upgrade to first-class on your next trip or perhaps purchase an outfit from a high-end store to be the essence of the person you are aiming to become?

These actions may appear small, but they serve as vital stepping stones, conditioning you for the life you're striving to create.

Ideal Experiences

1._____

_____

2._____

_____

3._____

_____

4._____

_____

5._____

_____

6._____

_____

7._____

_____

8._____

_____

9._____

_____

10._____

_____

Now, make a plan to go and experience these. When will you go? Put a date next to them. Then, sprinkle in moments throughout the next 30-90 days to explore and experience them.

You must intentionally craft your ideal life by taking a moment to pause and complete these exercises so they can serve as a starting point towards crafting more big audacious goals.

Chapter 3

Starting with Your Why

"Greatness is remembering in the dark what God told you in the light."

There will be challenging moments on your journey towards achieving your goal. It may feel tough and difficult and make you want to quit. However, it's important to remember that staying motivated and having a strong desire to pursue your goal is key to keep going. It's easy to give up when you're at your lowest point, feeling like you should just walk away and forget about it. You might even question why you started in the first place. It may feel like you need a life jacket, but waiting until you're already in the deep end screaming for help is too late.

Even a brand-new car comes equipped with a spare tire tucked away in the trunk, a silent promise of reassurance. It's not something you think about as you drive that pristine vehicle off the dealership lot, basking in the sheen of its fresh paint and the smell of new upholstery. However, the spare is there for a reason: to get you back on the road should you unexpectedly hit a pothole or puncture a tire on a stray nail. It's your contingency plan, your safety net, that keeps you moving toward your destination.

Similarly, your "why" serves as your life's spare tire, a deeply rooted motivation that's crucial for navigating the bumps and obstacles on your journey. When circumstances turn challenging, and you're tempted to give up, your "why" is what will keep you going. It isn't just an add-on to your goal-setting process; it's the cornerstone that gives your objectives meaning and momentum. Your "why" offers the emotional and psychological traction needed to reach not just the goals you set but to achieve them in a way that adds fulfillment and purpose to your life.

As you work towards your goal, you'll likely run into some tough spots that'll test your will to keep going. It's super important to have that motivation in your back pocket from the start—you can't just look for it when you're already in a jam. Think of it this way: The moment you set a goal, you're basically sending out an invitation for challenges to come and find you. The bigger and bolder your goal, the more life might start throwing curveballs your way.

In my faith, I've come to see this as God letting both you and the devil in on what you're up to. It's like the devil gets a notification the moment you decide to aim high. And trust me, he'll pull out all the stops to get in your way, throwing temptations, distractions, and all sorts of roadblocks at you.

But here's the thing: Those setbacks could end up working for you, even if you can't see it right then and there. It's like they're tests or lessons that, in the long run, make you stronger and more ready for what's next. Sure, you'll feel like throwing in the towel sometimes, but that's exactly when you need to dig deep and keep pushing. Don't turn your back on what you're after. Stick with it, and you'll see that all these challenges were just stepping stones on your way to something great.

Once you set a goal, understand that trials are likely to appear almost immediately. One of my mentors, Ash Cash, taught me, "There is always disruption before intention." It is as if the universe conducts a stress test the moment you make up your mind to pursue a goal. Suddenly, life throws unexpected hurdles your way—maybe a loved one passes away, pulling your focus and sapping your will to continue. Or perhaps your computer contracts a virus just when you have decided to start a web design business – how ironic. Or your car might decide to break down on your way to a life-changing job interview. These aren't mere coincidences; they are life's way of asking, "How badly do you want this?"

When you hit those rough patches and contemplate quitting, that's when your motivation and your "why" come into play. They serve as your lifelines, pulling you back on track when you're veering off course. Your "why" isn't just something to help you set a goal; it's the crucial factor that could very well determine whether or not you achieve it. So when times get tough, lean into your "why" and let it recenter and refuel you. It has the power to turn setbacks into setups for future success.

Simon Sinek, a renowned author and inspirational speaker, emphasized the significance of the philosophy of starting with the why in his TED Talk. He introduced the Golden Circle concept, which includes the what, how, and why. Many successful organizations use this concept, including myself, when I worked at Turner Broadcasting. We utilized the Golden Circle to define our goals, purpose, mission, values, and objectives for the year ahead.

The Golden Circle also helped me understand what goals I wanted to achieve, why I wanted to achieve them, and how I could achieve them. The most challenging part of goal setting is starting with the what, which is the clearest, but also the result they are striving for. Successful companies, however, reverse the process and start with the why, which is the inner core. When the company is clear on its "why", it tends to be more successful, not just in terms of profits but also in understanding its purpose and executing it, this not only resonates with the employees but also with the customers.

Breaking down the Golden Circle, the outer portion of the circle is the how, which determines how the end result will be accomplished. The next inner layer is the what, which specifies what the company wants to achieve. The innermost circle is the why, which serves as the purpose or belief set by the company. It is crucial to operate from the inside out; otherwise, the goal will not be hit. The why serves as the motivation that provides the utmost focus on the specific goal being pursued.

Understanding the reason behind something is crucial as it serves three primary purposes: intrinsic motivation, sustainability, and clarity/focus. Intrinsic motivation is the internal drive that is often stronger than external factors and is not visible to the naked eye. The "why" is what ignites this motivation within you. It's a deep internal force that you can feel and know, driving your desire to achieve your goals.

The next factor to consider is sustainability. Knowing your purpose will make your efforts more sustainable in the long term. So, when faced with challenges, keep in mind that your purpose can provide the endurance you need to continue. Lastly, clarity and focus are essential. Explaining the reasons behind your purpose can help you avoid distractions and stay focused on your ultimate objectives. This makes the journey towards your goals more efficient and effective. Therefore, keeping these three components in mind will help you understand the direction and guidance you need to achieve your goals. I can break it down further by helping you understand the driving force behind every goal. There are three core examples I want to share with you to make it more realistic. First, personal values often serve as an underlying purpose and shape the goals you set for yourself.

In the movie "The Pursuit of Happyness," starring Will Smith and his son Jaden Smith, Will Smith portrays the real-life person Chris Gardner. Gardner, a self-made millionaire, started as a salesman and became a stockbroker before eventually becoming a philanthropist.

The movie depicts a poignant scene where Gardner hit rock bottom and found himself sleeping in the basement of a subway bathroom. He struggled to make ends meet, hustling to sell medical equipment while trying to provide for his son. Despite the challenges, Gardner persevered and eventually found a mentor who helped him achieve his goal of becoming a professional stockbroker. He passed the Series 7 exam and gained employment at a firm, rising to success and eventually selling his own firm, Gardner Rich & Company. He became a well-known figure in the black community, inspiring others to pursue their dreams and never give up. Gardner's story reminds us that we are only down and out as long as we allow ourselves to be, and with hard work and determination, we can achieve our goals and surpass our limitations.

The next one is emotional connection is vital in achieving one's goals. The role of emotional connection in achieving your goals cannot be overstated. This deep attachment to a specific objective fuels your motivation to go above and beyond. When someone's well-being hinges on your actions, you're naturally propelled to give your utmost effort day in and day out. A compelling example of this principle in action is the story of Eric Thomas, also known as ET, the renowned motivational speaker.

When ET's wife was diagnosed with multiple sclerosis (MS), a condition that affects the central nervous system, their world turned upside down. Medical advice indicated she could no longer continue her work as a nurse, effectively making ET the sole provider for their family. To make matters more challenging, her condition required a higher vitamin D intake, mainly through sunlight, to mitigate potential worsening symptoms. At the time, they were living in Lansing, Michigan, where the sun was limited with long periods of widespread and long-lasting overcasts.

Confronted by these circumstances, ET made a bold and life-changing decision: he relocated his family from Lansing, Michigan, to San Diego, California, to take advantage of the more favorable climate for his wife's health. The move also came with a specific financial objective—affording an $11,000 mortgage payment. ET wanted to provide a dream house for his wife that would be comfortable and conducive to his ideal dream home. To achieve this, ET ramped up his speaking engagements, not just to cover the high cost of living but to ensure that his wife would never have to work again.

ET's "why" was profoundly personal and emotionally charged: it was his love and responsibility for his family. This emotional connection served as a powerful motivator, driving him to surmount obstacles and achieve his ambitious goals. So, as you formulate your own goals, consider the emotional connection that can serve as your "fuel," giving you the resilience and determination you need to succeed.

The final element worth considering is the impact of social and cultural factors on your "why." While societal expectations and cultural norms can shape your motivations, the key is to ensure that your "why" remains deeply personal and authentic, uninfluenced by external pressures. A compelling example of this is Dr. Martin Luther King, Jr., a man who defied all conventional wisdom and societal norms to become an icon of change. How did one man manage to accomplish something so groundbreaking?

It wasn't as though Dr. King was the only individual to suffer under the injustices of pre-civil rights America. Nor was he the sole gifted orator of his era. So why him? Why was he the one who rose above insurmountable odds to lead a transformative movement? The answer lies in the power of his "why": he had a dream.

Dr. King's dream wasn't just a lofty ideal; it was a deeply ingrained motivation that propelled him to act, even when faced with overwhelming obstacles. His "why" wasn't swayed by the societal expectations of his time; rather, it resonated at a personal level that transcended these pressures. So, as you navigate your own journey, remember the importance of having a "why" that is authentically yours, one that can empower you to rise above any challenges, just as Dr. King did.

What fuels your drive to chase after your most ambitious goals? Understanding your "why" is crucial—it's the driving force that will sustain your efforts day in and day out. Life is full of challenges that can easily discourage you and make you want to throw in the towel. However, a well-defined "why" will serve as your internal alarm clock, naturally waking you up and compelling you to forge ahead. Achieving your dream will require sacrifices and audacious steps, and you'll need to hold yourself accountable to stay on course. Once your driving forces are clearly identified, there will be virtually no stopping you from pursuing your aspirations. To help you unearth these pivotal motivations, I'll offer a range of exercises designed to probe deeper into what truly moves you.

Try one of the three exercises below to help you understand your why. If you're feeling ambitious, complete all three exercises. You never know which one will really help you to discover the real reason why you are pursuing the goal.

The 5 Whys Exercise: Ask yourself "Why?" five consecutive times to dig deeper into the root cause or true motivation behind your goal.

1. **WHY:**

_____
_____
_____
_____
_____
_____
_____
_____
_____
_____
_____
_____
_____

2. **WHY:**

_____

_____
_____
_____
_____
_____
_____
_____
_____
_____
_____
_____
_____
_____
_____

3. **WHY:**

_____
_____
_____
_____
_____
_____
_____
_____
_____
_____
_____
_____
_____
_____

4. **WHY:**

_____

5. **WHY:**

Write responses to the two journal prompts below:

1. **What impact do you want to leave on the world?**

_____
_____
_____
_____
_____
_____
_____
_____
_____
_____
_____
_____
_____
_____
_____
_____

2. **How would achieving this goal change your life for the better?**

_____
_____
_____
_____
_____
_____
_____
_____

_____

_____

_____

_____

_____

_____

_____

_____

Vision-Alignment Exercise:

Visualize your life after achieving your goal, and jot down the feelings and thoughts that come up. Spend at least 20 minutes thinking and visualizing it. This will help you to really solidify your "Why."

_____

_____

_____

_____

_____

_____

_____

_____

_____

_____

_____

_____

_____

_____

_____

_____

_____

_____

_____

_____

_____

_____

_____

Understanding your "Why" is a critical first step in any meaningful journey toward achieving big audacious goals. Without fully understanding your motives, you will lose focus and get distracted on the journey. Take the time to deeply explore your motivations. This will help you to navigate your path to success. Don't skip this part of the process!

Chapter 4

Crafting a Vision for Your Life

In the Bible, Habakkuk 2:2-3 teaches us the importance of living by faith. Scripture reads, "Write the vision; make it plain on tablets, so he may run who reads it. 3 For still the vision awaits its appointed time; it hastens to the end—it will not lie. If it seems slow, wait for it; it will surely come; it will not delay."

Crafting a vision for your life is biblical and it is a key component of achieving your goal. Faith is everything, especially when it comes to going after something that is audacious. The trials and tribulations you will face will create doubt and wariness, but you can't lose hope.

Vision serves as a long-term roadmap, guiding your daily actions and decisions. You will experience speed bumps, roadblocks, and even moments when you feel like you are in the HOV lane. But along the way, you could be distracted by the scenery and other exits. However, you can't get distracted. Stay the course and focus on the ultimate goal.

In this chapter, I will teach you how to take your why and your goal to create a vision for where you're seeking to go.

First, let's start with the purpose of a vision.

The vision will serve you throughout the journey. Without a clear vision, people perish, and without a vision, you will not have direction. The vision will help you to stay focused and bypass the distractions. Trust me, you will need a vision. You can get off track sooner than you think. In a world overflowing with options and distractions, having a vision keeps you on track, helping you navigate life's complexities with a sense of direction.

One of the key elements I used to help major companies define their strategy was to start with the vision. The vision provided the destination for the company. It guides not only the organization but also the people within the organization.

Having a clear vision for your life functions like a compass, guiding you through the labyrinth of choices and opportunities you face daily. It establishes a long-term trajectory, adding a sense of purpose to each step you take. This is not about merely "going through the motions" or reacting to life as it comes at you; it's about proactive living. Each decision and each action becomes a purposeful stride toward a destiny you've chosen.

Your vision becomes the framework within which you operate, infusing your daily routines with intention and driving you toward a life that reflects your deepest values and desires. The vision you create could serve your family and the team you may need to help you execute your goals. If you cannot clearly articulate your vision, you will have a tough time aligning yourself with the people and resources you need to achieve your goals.

The vision will also inspire and motivate you to keep going when things get tough. On those mornings when you question the point of getting out of bed, your vision serves as a compelling reason, nudging you into action because you know there's a bigger narrative you're contributing to.

I recall when I was looking for my first investment property. It took eight months before I was able to put in my first offer. Then, it was another six months before I closed on my first property. I had to get myself financially positioned; I needed to secure all the right legal documentation and the right team to make it all come together. When I finally got it, I was exhausted. But this was just the beginning of a long road ahead. I had hit a major milestone of purchasing the property, but I had no idea what awaited me. I had moments when I wanted to give up or thought investing wasn't for me, but I held on to the vision. And I committed to it, knowing that my opportunity would eventually come.

Focusing on my vision of becoming a real estate investor was the emotional fuel when times got tough for me. The emotions I was experiencing created the passion and the excitement to keep going because I knew with each step I was getting closer and closer to the goal. The mundane tasks became meaningful each day.

My vision served as an endless source of inspiration and motivation. Unlike fleeting bursts of enthusiasm, a vision is a well from which you can draw when your initial motivation dies, when you experience setbacks, or when you simply have moments of doubt. It acts as a mental and emotional reservoir, filling you with the energy needed to overcome challenges and continue moving forward.

It's the resilience you need when you face challenges or setbacks. Your vision becomes your sanctuary to reground you, helping you bounce back and renew your focus and commitment. I would pray to God and literally say to God, "I know this is temporary, and I know I will get through these small beginnings, but I know the steps I can take now will only get me closer to the vision. Help me to stay focused and believe this is possible for me."

When the vision is well-crafted, it isn't just for the short-term; it's for the long term, and it helps you achieve your ultimate vision for your life. It even provides the enduring motivation that makes it easier to sacrifice immediate gratification for long-term success. Your vision will outlast the small goals but creates the big picture for the life you desire.

Decision Making

Your vision serves as an invaluable compass for decision-making, setting the gold standard against which you weigh all opportunities and choices that cross your path. Whether you're pondering a career shift, assessing a potential partnership, or debating various life choices, your vision acts as the ultimate filter.

In the maze of life's options, your vision provides immediate clarity. It enables you to discern whether a given opportunity will align with your long-term objectives and enrich your well-being or divert you off course. Asking yourself, "Does this choice align with my vision?" can be remarkably clarifying. A "yes" invites careful consideration; a "no" allows for swift elimination, saving you from wasting energy on incongruent pursuits.

This clarity streamlines your decision-making process. Instead of drowning in endless pros and cons, your vision offers a single, unambiguous metric: does this choice serve my ultimate life goals? It alleviates the cognitive burden and emotional strain often associated with major decisions, allowing you to focus on what truly matters.

But the utility of your vision doesn't stop at providing a guideline; it also serves as a risk assessment tool. With a well-articulated vision, you become more intuitive in evaluating potential benefits and drawbacks. You'll find it easier to step out of your comfort zone when a promising opportunity arises that aligns with your greater aspirations.

So, what makes a vision effective in bringing this level of clarity? A well-defined vision is like a high-resolution roadmap, offering explicit directions without room for doubt or misinterpretation. The clearer your vision, the more explicit your objectives become, making them easier to pursue and measure. Such clarity not only simplifies your journey but also bolsters your confidence, making it easier to gain support from others without the need for elaborate explanations.

In sum, a clear and aligned vision reduces decision-making complexity and cognitive load, allowing you to focus and act with purpose. It becomes the guiding pulse of your life, dictating the steps you take, the risks you assume, and the choices you make, ensuring every action is a step toward your ultimate destination.

Elements of a Strong Vision

A robust vision ignites passion, serving as the emotional fuel necessary for the long-haul effort to realize your dreams. When your vision is suffused with passion, your path feels less like an obligation and more like an exhilarating journey toward a fulfilling life. This passion transforms your vision into a calling, organically pulling you toward it each day and becoming an integral part of your identity.

In doing so, passion makes the challenges, sacrifices, and hard work worth the effort, transforming your labor into a labor of love. This emotional investment not only sustains your journey but also serves as a catalyst that propels you through inevitable obstacles. When you're driven by intrinsic motivation—a passion that comes from within, independent of external rewards—the journey itself becomes the reward.

Passion acts like an internal battery pack, supercharging your actions and imbuing your daily tasks with enthusiasm and vigor. This heightened energy minimizes procrastination and self-doubt, fostering a laser-focused drive to achieve your vision.

When your vision is in harmony with your values, utilizes your skills, and resonates with your life's circumstances and aspirations, it's not just compelling but also realistic and sustainable. Such an alignment taps into the 'why' that drives you, which we've explored in previous chapters, creating a trifecta of sustainability, synergy, and authenticity.

Sustainability: An aligned vision can be maintained over the long term because it seamlessly integrates with who you are and who you aspire to be.

Synergy: When your vision resonates with your skills and values, a synergistic effect occurs, where each component amplifies the other, making your path more coherent and your efforts more impactful.

Authenticity: An aligned vision that feels genuinely yours creates a deeper level of commitment. You're not chasing someone else's dream or yielding to societal pressures; you're pursuing what genuinely matters to you.

These three core components intersect to define the potency of your vision. By optimizing each, you craft a compelling, actionable, and transformative vision that can guide you to a fulfilling life.

Chapter 5

Crafting Your Vision Statement

Let's spend time crafting your vision. This is internal work, but it will be worth it! Let's go through this process by following the tips below.

Start Broad, Then Narrow Down

Begin by writing down broad phrases or sentences that encapsulate the overall feeling or direction of your vision. At this point, don't worry about precision or word choice; just focus on capturing the essence.

Use Action Words

Vision statements are more compelling when they're dynamic. Use action verbs to give your vision movement and direction. For example, instead of saying, "I want to be a writer," you might say, "I will captivate audiences with storytelling."

Identify Key Themes

Review what you've written and identify recurring themes or elements. Are there particular values, goals, or concepts that appear repeatedly? Highlight these for further refinement.

Be Clear and Specific

This is the point where you begin to clarify what your vision entails. Revisit the answers to your "why" exercises in the previous chapter.

Incorporate the Emotional Element

A vision is not just an intellectual exercise; it should stir emotions. Use emotive words to articulate not just what you will do or achieve but how it will feel. For instance, instead of saying, "I will be financially independent," you could say, "I will live a life free from financial stress, filled with choices and opportunities."

Make it Concise but Comprehensive

Aim for brevity without sacrificing completeness. Your vision statement should be concise enough to be memorable but comprehensive enough to guide your decisions and give you direction.

Craft Multiple Versions

It's often useful to create long, medium, and short versions of your vision statement. The long version can be a paragraph that provides a full overview. The medium version can be a sentence or two that captures the essence. The short version can be a phrase or motto that acts as a quick reminder of your vision.

Let It Sit, Then Revise

After your initial draft, step away for a bit— maybe a day or two—then come back and read it again. You'll often see ways to improve clarity, remove redundancy, or add missing elements.

Your initial draft may not feel quite right, and that's okay. The point is to start putting your vision into words so that it can be refined, shared, and, ultimately, realized.

To help, below is an example of a vision statement with supporting details of why it is a solid vision statement to model:

"In five years, I envision my coffee shop as the heartbeat of our community—a sanctuary of warmth, creativity, and connection. Rooted in ethical sourcing and sustainability, our café will serve not just exceptional coffee but also be a platform for local artists and musicians. Our welcoming space will inspire authentic conversations, foster meaningful relationships, and serve as an inclusive haven for people from all walks of life. Through our products, customer service, and community outreach, we will redefine what it means to be a coffee shop, emphasizing the importance of coming together as a community to share in the simple yet profound joys of life."

Key Features:

- The vision statement emphasizes community engagement and aims to be more than just a place to get coffee.
- It highlights ethical and sustainable practices in sourcing coffee and other products.

- The vision extends to supporting local talents like artists and musicians, making it a multi-purpose space.
- It touches on inclusivity and diversity, making the coffee shop welcoming for everyone.
- This vision serves as a foundational guide, setting the tone for the unique, community-centered, and ethical coffee shop the owner aspires to create.

This vision serves as a foundational guide, setting the tone for the unique, community-centered, and ethical coffee shop the owner aspires to create.

Once the vision is set then you can create the mission. This will be the guiding light to get to the ultimate destination – the goal.

Use the space below to start crafting your vision statement. Your vision statement can be as detailed as you desire – it is your vision. But I would challenge you to make a second variation of the vision statement that is clear and concise enough for you to be able to recall it. Here is a second iteration of the same vision statement:

"In five years, my coffee shop will be the community's sanctuary for warmth, creativity, and connection, emphasizing ethical sourcing, sustainability, and fostering meaningful relationships through art, music, and authentic conversations."

Detailed Vision Statement:

_____

_____

_____

_____

_____

_____

_____

_____

_____

_____

_____

_____

_____

_____

_____

_____

_____

_____

_____

_____

_____

_____

Brief Vision Statement:

_____

_____

_____

_____

_____

_____

Chapter 6

Power of Visualization

We're ready to dive straight into the goal-setting process, but there's more groundwork to cover first. This foundational work, the pre-planning and preparation, is crucial. I promise it's not just busy work – it's the foundation for everything else.

There is another technique that is insanely invaluable along the way to achieving your goal – Visualization. It is a fascinating concept of human psychology that can help you realize your goal faster.

Having a vision statement is like having a map in your back pocket. It points you in the right direction. But visualization? That's the GPS that talks to you, reminding you of every turn.

Visualization is the practice of using one's imagination to create a mental image or scenario to achieve a goal. It's a technique often used to mentally rehearse actions, simulate different outcomes, and focus your thoughts on achieving a specific goal. It is the process of training your subconscious mind. You're probably wondering what I mean by training your subconscious mind – that's a completely different book.

At its essence, the subconscious mind is a deep well of thoughts, memories, experiences, and convictions existing just beneath our active awareness. It silently operates in the background, handling much of the information our conscious mind doesn't directly address. The subconscious significantly shapes our behavior, as our deeply held beliefs influence our automatic reactions and habits. This makes it crucial to align the subconscious with our goals, ensuring it aids rather than hinders your journey toward your goals.

Visualization can be used to "program" the subconscious mind. By consistently feeding it with positive images and thoughts about our goals, we condition ourselves to act in ways that make those aspirations a reality. This is why athletes, performers, and successful professionals often employ visualization techniques – to prime their subconscious for success.

Athletes frequently employ dynamic techniques for mental preparation leading up to significant games. They often visualize triumphant moments, like landing the winning shot or hearing the crowd's exhilaration after a last-second score.

A notable example is LeBron James, who was captured on live TV, meditating on the sidelines before a crucial game, as his teammates warmed up. This meditation is a staple in LeBron's pregame ritual. Recognizing that success in the game is half mental, he even enlisted the expertise of a sports psychologist to fortify his mental game. He understands the need to balance physical prowess with mental readiness.

The same technique can be used to help you visualize achieving your goal. Pairing this technique with visual cues from your vision board and your vision statement can fortify your goals.

It can enhance your motivation and boost your confidence. When you can 'see' the finish line, the hurdles along the way appear surmountable, pushing you to strive harder towards your goals. Visualizing yourself successfully achieving a goal can provide a significant confidence boost.

The habit of visualizing also creates an interesting way of "visiting your goal" and the ability to experience your desired goal before you actualize it. When you have a vivid image in your mind of what you wish to achieve, it becomes easier to outline the actionable steps required to reach that outcome. It essentially acts as a mental rehearsal for the real task, preparing you both mentally and emotionally.

Though not strictly scientific, many people believe that visualization activates the Law of Attraction, thereby drawing your desires towards you. While the empirical evidence for this is limited, the optimistic mental state fostered by positive visualization can undoubtedly make you more receptive to opportunities that align with your goals.

Let's walk through the process of how you can effectively practice visualization.

First, find a quiet and comfortable space where you can focus without distractions. Relax your body and mind through deep breathing. As you enter a relaxed state, vividly imagine your vision coming to life, engaging as many of your senses as possible. Try to feel the emotions you would experience upon realizing your vision, as emotional involvement enhances the impact of visualization. Instead of imagining a static scene, make your visualization dynamic, incorporating motion and sequence to make it more lifelike.

Really embrace and feel the experience as if you are already there. Who is there? What are you doing? What are you saying? What are you wearing? How are people responding to you? How do you feel? Stay in the state as long as you can and just be present in the moment. Ignore any distractions in the physical room and just be. Try to stay in the moment for at least 10 – 20 minutes to get the full effect, but stop whenever you see fit.

Use your visualization sessions as a springboard to take real steps toward your goal and make adjustments to your mental blueprint as you make progress. This comprehensive approach not only makes your visualization more vivid but also integrates it seamlessly into your action plan for achieving your objectives. Consistency is key, so try to practice visualization daily. However, don't forget that while visualization is a powerful motivator, it's not a substitute for action.

Visualize your desires multiple times a day in the morning, afternoon, and evening. The intention is to visualize it as often as possible to begin to feel and see your vision as clearly as possible and to train your mind to see and feel it as clearly as possible.

Exercise: Take 20 minutes to sit in a comfortable position and visualize it. After you visualize it, take a few minutes and jot down how this made you feel. What was your experience like? How did this experience impact you?

_____
_____
_____
_____
_____
_____
_____
_____
_____
_____
_____
_____
_____
_____
_____
_____
_____
_____
_____
_____
_____
_____
_____
_____
_____
_____
_____

Chapter 7

Setting Your Goal

Let's dive in and move closer to realizing our big audacious goal. While you've done a commendable job visualizing and understanding the profound impact of your aspirations, the next step is pivotal: breaking your goal into tangible chunks. Think of it as slicing your vision into 90-day segments, manageable yet meaningful. And the S.M.A.R.T. Goals Framework is your best tool for this. It not only sharpens the focus on your objectives but also lays down a clear path for the next three months. With this approach, you won't just dream; you'll actualize your ambitions.

The framework has been instrumental in guiding my goal-setting process. Every year, I set a specific goal to achieve, marking my progress with 90-day benchmarks. 2022 stands out as a year where I achieved some truly ambitious goals. These 90-day increments acted as essential milestones that kept me on track.

In the first quarter of that year, I successfully flipped a single-family home in Chicago, despite it being out of state for me. By the second quarter, I ventured into investing in an out-of-state restaurant, which subsequently opened doors for me to become an angel investor. In the third quarter, I purchased my first home, a four-unit building. I embraced the house hacking strategy: living in one unit while renting out the others. Then, in the fourth quarter, I launched the "One Day" brand.

This brand emphasizes assisting people in achieving their big, audacious goals. Many aspire to realize "one day, someday" dreams but fail to act. The "One Day" brand provides tools and products to assist individuals not only in setting their aspirations but also in ensuring they stay accountable and achieve them.

That year was transformative for me, marked by unwavering focus and commitment. The strategies I share in this book are the very ones I applied to accomplish all I did in just that single year. I'm here to guide you through these processes, ensuring you execute at an elevated level. We'll kick things off with the S.M.A.R.T. framework, delving into each component in detail. By the end of this chapter, you'll have a concrete S.M.A.R.T. goal ready to propel you through your next 90 days.

S.M.A.R.T. Goals Framework

Specific: Setting a goal that is clear and specific is crucial to its success. Being specific gives a clear sense of direction and provides a benchmark against which progress can be measured. A vague goal is hard to act on.

Instead of saying, "I want passive income," a specific goal could be, "I want to net $10,000 in monthly passive income."

Measurable: If you can't measure it, you can't manage it. A measurable goal has clear criteria that allow you to track your progress. This makes it easier to monitor how close or far you are from achieving your goal. For example, if your goal is to get to $10,000 in monthly passive income, you can set a benchmark to assess progress towards the goal, like, "Every year I will acquire one asset that will net me at least $2,000 in monthly passive income."

Achievable: Goals should be challenging but still within the realms of possibility. If a goal is set too high, it may seem unattainable, leading to discouragement. If it's set too low, it won't be motivating. While goals should push you, they shouldn't be so unrealistic that they demotivate you. Ensure that with effort and dedication, the goal is attainable. If you said, "I want to be a millionaire in one year," it might be possible, but is it realistic from where you're starting? But, if you have a goal that puts you in a position to become a millionaire in net worth in 5 years, then maybe it can be obtained with time. The idea is to be realistic based on your starting point.

Relevant: Your goal should align with your broader life ambitions and the vision you outlined in the previous chapter. If you envisioned yourself being a real estate investor, but the goal you set is focusing on starting a trucking business or a health goal, you are not focusing on a relevant goal. The goal you set should align with the vision you desire.

Time-bound: Every goal should have a deadline. Time constraints create urgency and spur motivation. Instead of saying, "I want to net $10,000 in monthly passive income," you could say, "In 5 years, I will net $10,000 in monthly passive income." The deadline acts as a motivator and provides a timeframe within which progress can be measured.

To clearly define your goal, it can be written as:

"In 5 years, I will net $10,000 in monthly passive income. Every year, I will commit to acquiring at least one income-producing asset that nets $2,000 or more in monthly passive income."

When your goal is clear and specific, it eliminates any uncertainty about what you aim to accomplish. This clarity provides direction and sharpens your focus, guiding the commitment you're prepared to make.

Take a moment to write your S.M.A.R.T. goal
below:

_____
_____
_____
_____
_____
_____
_____
_____
_____
_____
_____

The goal you've penned down is a beacon,
guiding you closer to the life painted in your
vision statement. But imagine if we refined this
even further. How could we distill this goal into
specific milestones to hit over the next 90
days? Milestones that inch you closer to that
dream.

You might wonder, "Why specifically 90 days?"
Well, the year is divided into four quarters,
each spanning roughly 90 days. By segmenting
your goal across these quarters, it becomes not
only more digestible but also more achievable.
This quarterly breakdown lets you track your
daily progress over 13 weeks, making the
journey palpable and the milestones visible.

Zeroing in on the upcoming 90 days provides clarity. It outlines precise tasks that must be tackled in this relatively short window, making the goal feel both achievable and grounded. Conversely, if we only gaze at the distant horizon, our goal might seem elusive and the path to it a tad hazy, leading to uncertainty in our daily actions.

For instance using the earlier example, if the goal is acquiring an income-producing asset, a proximate objective might be setting aside a certain sum of money. Without the requisite funds, the larger goal remains a mirage. Hence, I might either focus on saving diligently or explore inventive avenues to amass the needed capital.

This is how I would draft a 90-day goal to support my 5-year objective of generating $10,000 in monthly passive income. Assuming it's January 2024 when I'm setting this goal, my 90-day target would be:

"I will acquire the necessary knowledge and financial resources required to obtain my first asset-producing property by March 30th."

This goal emphasizes the importance of researching the requirements to acquire an asset. It could also help you assess your finances to see how much you need to save. Alternatively, it might encourage you to consult a financial advisor to better prepare for the purchase. For the upcoming 90 days, until

March 30th, direct all your energy towards learning and strategizing. With this intense focus, you'll be well-prepared to buy an asset by year's end.

Now you try. Create your 90-Day goal below:

_____

_____

_____

_____

_____

_____

_____

_____

_____

_____

_____

_____

_____

_____

_____

_____

_____

_____

_____

_____

_____

_____

_____

To guide you on this journey towards your 90-day goal, I recommend acquiring the "One Day" Daily Execution Planner available at www.theoneday.co. This planner offers step-by-step guidance to document your aspirations and presents reflective prompts tailored for your initial 90-Day objective. Let's delve into these prompts.

1. **"This goal is important to me because…"**: Delve deep into the rationale behind your goal. This reflection often reconnects you with the overarching vision you've set. Perhaps this goal propels you closer to that vision. By understanding and acknowledging the importance of this goal, you establish a firmer commitment, ensuring you're driven to reach not just this goal, but subsequent ones too.

2. **"When I achieve this goal, my life will…"**: Envision the transformative impact of accomplishing your goal. How will it reshape your current circumstances or elevate your life? Articulating these changes helps cement the goal's significance.

3. **"To achieve this goal, I am willing to sacrifice…"**: Every meaningful goal demands sacrifices, be it time, money, or occasionally, peace of mind. Recognize what you're prepared

to give up to bring your vision to life. This sacrifice is often a testament to your dedication. Remember, growth requires change. To attain new goals, sometimes we must evolve or adjust our aspirations. Clarify for yourself: what will you forgo or adapt to make your dream a reality?

4. **"When I achieve this goal, I will celebrate by..."**: Think about your victory lap even as you immerse yourself in the rigors of relentless work and focus, earmarking moments for celebration. Recognizing your achievements fuels motivation and breaks the monotony, keeping you inspired and energized for future endeavors.

Contemplating these four statements after delineating your goal adds depth to your commitment. While it might appear overwhelming, this groundwork shields you during challenging times. These reflections act as a beacon, illuminating your path when obstacles cloud your way. This preparatory phase is essential, equipping you with resilience and clarity for the journey ahead.

You can document your responses in the book, or you can document them in the planner.

1. **"This goal is important to me because...":**

_____
_____
_____
_____
_____
_____
_____
_____
_____
_____
_____
_____
_____
_____

2. **"When I achieve this goal, my life will...":**

_____
_____
_____
_____
_____
_____
_____
_____
_____
_____
_____
_____
_____
_____

_____

_____

_____

_____

_____

_____

_____

_____

_____

_____

_____

3. **"To achieve this goal, I am willing to sacrifice...":**

_____

_____

_____

_____

_____

_____

_____

_____

_____

_____

_____

_____

_____

_____

_____

_____

_____

_____

_____

_____

_____

_____

_____

_____

4. **"When I achieve this goal, I will celebrate by...":**

_____

_____

_____

_____

_____

_____

_____

_____

_____

_____

_____

_____

_____

_____

_____

_____

_____

_____

_____

Chapter 8

Achieving Your Goal

Are you ready to dive deep into the actionable steps to achieve your goals? The time has finally come. So far, you have thoroughly dissected your vision, examined your goals, and reflected deeply on the strategic efforts required to reach your goals. This foundational work sets the stage for a precise goal roadmap and an actionable execution plan.

We're now ready to start executing. Taking that first, bold step toward any goal can be intimidating. The fear of the unknown can paralyze many, causing stagnation. However, the magic happens when you send that first email, take that initial step, or introduce yourself to a mentor. That's when opportunities unfold. Remember, as Lao Tzu aptly said, "The journey of a thousand miles begins with a single step."

But which step do I take, and how do I tackle it? I got you! I will introduce you to the concept of milestones and tasks to achieve your goal. With my background as a project manager, I've aided Fortune 500 companies in their ambitious ventures. The tactics I share are the same as those employed by industry leaders and executives. Fortune 500 companies struggle to figure it out too, so don't worry, you are not alone. The real secret is they hire consultants like me from the Big 4 consulting firms to help them. Now, I'll teach you the exact same concepts.

First, it is crucial to decompose your overarching goal. This segmentation reduces feelings of being overwhelmed. Your goal can seem distant and unattainable, and if you don't know what to do, you will procrastinate or settle for the familiar. However, true triumphs come from confronting challenges head-on.

Imagine trying to knock down a large tree; you can't knock it down all in one single hit with an ax. But your consistent efforts, striking the same spot, will eventually bring it down. Or as they say when you're trying to eat an elephant, you can't eat it all at once. You have to break it down into bite-sized pieces – who is eating an elephant, really, but you get the idea.

These analogies capture our objective: fragmenting your goal into smaller, digestible portions, making attainment feel within reach. This methodical breakdown I offer will provide clarity, simplify the journey, and provide a comprehensive guide. It will help you to manage your goal, making it easier to schedule, delegate, or maneuver.

Let's begin by understanding the concept of a milestone. A **milestone** is a significant marker or event in the progression of your goal. It represents a notable achievement or stage of progress. Milestones can be thought of as markers that indicate how far along you are in your journey toward completing a specific goal. They do not, by themselves, constitute the actual work but instead signify the completion of certain batches of work.

Think of it as reaching a landmark during a cross-country trip. For instance, if you are driving from Baltimore to California, passing through specific states indicates how close you are to your destination. These landmarks serve as milestones, assuring you're on the right track.

To identify the milestones for your goal, think about the key marks you want to hit that will help you track substantial progress towards your goal.

For example, when I purchased the single-family property I flipped in 2022, my major milestones were:

1. Establishing a Limited Liability Company (LLC)
2. Creating a real estate team
3. Finding a property
4. Renovating the property
5. Selling the property

Every time I hit one of these milestones, I knew I was getting closer to completing the project and hitting my goal.

With each of these milestones, I had a set of tasks. **Tasks** are the steps you take to reach the milestone and eventually, your final goal. They are a specific unit of work required to achieve part of a larger goal. They are action-oriented and represent something that needs to be done or acted upon. Unlike milestones, tasks have a start and end time. They might take hours, days, or even weeks to complete, depending on the complexity.

For example, consider the process of writing a book. The completion of each chapter can be viewed as a milestone, while the sections or components within each chapter represent the tasks. Both milestones and tasks are instrumental in organizing and streamlining your journey towards goal attainment.

So, for the milestone of "Establishing a Limited Liability Company (LLC)", there were a handful of tasks I needed to complete:

1. Decide on a business name.
2. Establish a business address.
3. Designate a registered agent.
4. Prepare the LLC Articles of Organization Form to submit to the Secretary of State.
5. File the Articles of Organization.
6. Create an Operating Agreement.

To simplify the difference between a milestone and a task, consider this analogy: If you are on a road trip, the milestones might be the major cities or landmarks you pass, while the tasks are the turns, stops, and actions you take to get to each city or landmark.

When you start to identify your milestones and tasks it might be a little challenging, especially when it is your first time. You don't know where to begin and you don't know the first step to take. But keep this in mind: "Success leaves clues." In our digital age, with platforms like Google, Instagram, podcasts, artificial intelligence, and the vast resources of YouTube University, you're already surrounded by a wealth of knowledge. If you have never achieved the goal you are setting out to propose, I am sure there are tons of other people who have, and there is information everywhere. You just have to find the clues....

The clues are on YouTube, at a seminar, or even someone you meet at a networking event. Many cities, including their neighboring areas, host events, seminars, and workshops all the time. Even if it means catching a flight, seize the opportunity to connect with communities that are connected to your goal. Networking is invaluable. These connections can be pivotal in ensuring you're on the right trajectory and provide information that can help you figure out the key milestones and tasks you need to take. When I decided I wanted to do real estate, I was constantly tuned into podcasts such as Bigger Pockets, and I joined real estate communities such as Make Real Estate Real, The Multifamily Movement, and Earn Your Leisure. I tapped into these communities to learn the process and even met some pretty cool people along the way. Information will be critical to ensure you are identifying the right steps and the order of steps to follow.

Once you start making the right connections with people and you start making traction on your milestones and your tasks, this will give you the momentum to keep going.

Achieving milestones gives you the confidence to keep going and you will experience a significant psychological boost. This sense of accomplishment not only offers immediate gratification, which our human psyche craves, but it also instills confidence that propels us forward.

Within the Daily Execution Planner, I've designed a dedicated page to help you outline the major milestones necessary for reaching your goal. Initially, it may seem daunting to identify every task, but as you gather information and connect with mentors, your path will become clearer.

My goal is to assist you in breaking down your objectives into easily manageable steps. This is the essence of the Daily Execution Planner: ensuring you take actionable steps every day. With each day, you'll confidently check off tasks, inching closer to your goal.

Let's take a minute and start jotting down
some of your initial milestones and tasks:

Milestone:	Date:
Task #1:	
Task #2:	
Task #3:	
Task #4:	
Task #5:	

Milestone:	Date:
Task #1:	
Task #2:	
Task #3:	
Task #4:	
Task #5:	

Milestone:	Date:
Task #1:	
Task #2:	
Task #3:	
Task #4:	
Task #5:	

Milestone:	Date:
Task #1:	
Task #2:	
Task #3:	
Task #4:	
Task #5:	

Once you've identified your milestones, assign a date to each one. These dates act as benchmarks to gauge your progress. It's essential to set dates that reflect what you can realistically accomplish. Truly grasp both your capacity and the magnitude of what will be required to complete each milestone. To help in this, evaluate the tasks that make up the milestone and ask yourself: What is needed to complete this task? How much time will it require? Do I need assistance or support to finish it? Addressing these questions will guide you in determining what you can feasibly accomplish.

After identifying the dates for your milestones, take a calendar and mark those key dates. Use vibrant pens or color-code your tasks to make the process engaging and enjoyable. The Daily Execution Planner even features an undated monthly calendar, making it easy for you to jot down these crucial dates too.

Now, let's get to work!

Chapter 9

Time Management Techniques for Goal Crushers

Pinpointing your milestones and tasks are pivotal to transitioning from planning to action. The gap between knowledge and success often boils down to application. Merely possessing information doesn't equate to achievement; action does. I want to introduce you to four transformative time-management techniques that have been instrumental in my journey to consistently meet milestones and realize goals.

 While these techniques have been transformative for me, it's essential to find what resonates with you. Maybe it's one of these methods, a combination, or all four. Discover the rhythm that amplifies your productivity.

Time Block Method

The Time Block Method has been a game-changer for me, offering a strategy where you dedicate specific chunks of time to distinct tasks. Rather than navigating your day without a set plan, this method structures your hours into well-defined time slots, each reserved for a particular task or a set of related tasks. One of its standout advantages is the unwavering focus it provides. By zoning in on one task at a time, it keeps distractions at bay and curbs the temptation to multitask.

This method not only enhances your productivity but ensures a smooth transition between tasks with minimal downtime. It's like having a roadmap for your day, eliminating the paralysis of choice about which task to tackle next. Every task has its time, and you simply flow with it. Additionally, when a block of time is reserved for a task, it becomes an appointment you can't miss. This fosters a strong sense of commitment and accountability, making sure those tasks don't just linger on your to-do list. In essence, the Time Block Method is not just about managing tasks; it's about maximizing your day with purpose and intention.

To effectively implement the Time Block Method, start by listing the tasks you aim to complete for the day. Next, assess each task's duration; does it require 15 minutes, 30 minutes, or perhaps an hour? Once you've gauged the time needed, schedule specific blocks in your calendar or planner for each task. When the allotted time arrives, fully commit to working on that task.

For time blocking to truly be effective, be mindful of a few potential pitfalls. Firstly, always incorporate buffer periods between your time blocks to accommodate unexpected tasks and possible overflows. Refrain from overcommitting or setting overly ambitious schedules; this can be overwhelming and demoralizing when you don't achieve all your day's objectives. Also, be strategic about when you set these blocks. For instance, I dedicate 1 to 2 hours every morning before I go to work because after I get off from work, I often feel exhausted and am less productive. The morning proves to be my prime time for peak productivity. It's important that you also know your peak performance time; yours might be late at night, and that's fine too.

Additionally, it's crucial to minimize distractions during your time blocks. Consider setting your phone to 'do not disturb' mode or crafting an environment conducive to concentration. This not only enhances your focus but also curtails unnecessary interruptions. And remember, don't set exceedingly long time blocks. It's essential to allocate manageable durations that allow breaks, ensuring you neither burn out nor overextend yourself.

Art of Prioritization

Let's dive into the art of prioritization. The secret to effective task management is sorting them by importance. Allocate time every week to prioritize your array of tasks, guided by the following actions:

1. **Weekly Overview:** Jot down everything you intend to accomplish in the upcoming week. Think of this as a 'brain dump'— a space where you list out all anticipated tasks.
2. **Milestone Markers:** From this list, discern which tasks are pivotal for reaching your next milestone. Highlight these – maybe with a star or by circling them.
3. **The Top Trio:** From your highlighted tasks, zero in on the top three critical items. These are the tasks that should lead your week. Decide on specific days you'll tackle each.

Now, spread out the other tasks over the week, aiming to tackle 1 to 3 tasks daily. Importantly, pace yourself and avoid overburdening your schedule. To assist with this, the Daily Execution Planner offers a "Week at a Glance" feature, perfect for capturing your weekly priorities and daily action items.

Sprint

Enter the "sprint" - a dynamic concept borrowed from Agile methodologies widely used in corporate environments, particularly during significant product development or enhancement phases.

In essence, a sprint is a predetermined period, often spanning seven days, during which specific tasks are targeted for completion. Think of it as a concentrated, high-energy dash: for those seven days, you zero in exclusively on a designated task or set of tasks.

This approach is tailor-made for accomplishing milestones. Begin by evaluating your list of tasks, organizing them either sequentially or by priority. Choose the tasks you're dedicating the next seven days to, and for that duration, let them be your sole focus. This singular attention ensures you're not spreading yourself too thin or juggling multiple tasks haphazardly. The beauty of the sprint is its disciplined concentration, shielding you from the pitfalls of a scattered approach.

Quadrant Method

Prioritizing tasks can often feel overwhelming, but utilizing established methods can simplify the process. Another effective tool is Stephen Covey's 2x2 matrix, popularly known as the "quadrant method." This system provides a clear framework for classifying tasks based on urgency and importance.

Imagine a grid divided into four boxes.

Urgent and Important (Quadrant I): This is the "firefighting" quadrant. Tasks falling under this category require your immediate attention and action. They are often critical, time-sensitive, and cannot be postponed. Whether it's a looming deadline or an emergency, these tasks should be at the top of your to-do list.

Necessary but Not Urgent (Quadrant II): This quadrant is where planning and proactive measures lie. While these tasks aren't pressing, they're essential for long-term success. They should be scheduled for upcoming days or weeks, allowing you to address them methodically without the pressure of immediacy. This could include tasks like strategic planning or personal development activities.

Urgent but Not Important (Quadrant III): These tasks can be deceptive. They scream for attention due to their urgency, but in the grand scheme of things, they might not significantly contribute to your overarching goals. Delegating these tasks or seeking assistance can be beneficial, ensuring they're handled while freeing you to focus on more critical matters.

Neither Urgent nor Important (Quadrant IV): This quadrant is often filled with trivial tasks that might not have any significant impact. It's worth evaluating if these tasks need to be on your list at all. Can they be dropped or postponed indefinitely? Sometimes, what seems essential might just be a distraction.

By organizing tasks in this structured manner, you not only gain clarity on what needs immediate attention but also strategize for the future.

Each of these four methods has its merits, but the crux is selecting the one that resonates most with you and your goals. Hone in on that method and apply it diligently. You might already have a preferred technique, and that's okay. The essential thing is to choose a method that consistently drives your productivity and effectiveness.

Chapter 10:

Establishing a Productive Routine

My mentor once told me, "You can work your way into being unsuccessful with successful excuses." Permitting oneself to craft reasons for not meeting necessary tasks will undoubtedly hinder goal achievement. The cornerstone to ensuring success? A routine. Merely possessing the knowledge won't propel you towards your goal; your commitment and motivation play pivotal roles.

You must be accountable to yourself, prioritizing what's required to realize your aspirations. You owe it to yourself to hold yourself accountable. I am faithful to my routine. I was so committed to my routine that my friends and family knew it well. They would say, "I know it's almost 7 pm, and your phone will go to 'do not disturb,' but..." On one occasion, a friend voiced their frustration over my rigorous adherence, deeming me "overly structured." However, I recognize what propels me forward, and my disciplined routine was my personal accountability and the key to my success. Sometimes, prioritizing yourself may make others uncomfortable – they just don't get it.

A routine keeps me focused on my goals. Without it, I'm scattered, and my results show it. When I follow my routine daily, I see clear results, which boosts my confidence and drive. This feeling is like a personal reward. I've made a promise to myself to stick to my routine. Honestly, there were times I felt like breaking it, and when I did, I felt less accomplished. If life disrupted my routine, I'd ensure I returned to it within two days. If I ever changed my routine, it was only to improve it.

A routine is a requisite sacrifice, even if temporary. Eric Thomas once said, "Everybody wants to be successful until it's time to do what successful people do." – establish a routine.

A routine is a fixed sequence of actions or procedures that are followed regularly and consistently. It's a habitual or established series of tasks or activities that people often perform in the same way and at the same time, typically daily or weekly.

You may say, "I don't need a routine. It doesn't take all that." Oh, but it does. Let me explain how the brain works. There is neuroplasticity, also known as brain plasticity or neural plasticity. It refers to the brain's ability to reorganize itself, both in terms of its structure and how it functions in response to experience.

When we repeatedly perform a specific activity, our brain strengthens the neural pathways associated with that activity. Over time, these reinforced pathways make the activity become more automatic and easier to perform. This is the foundation of skill acquisition and habit formation.

Habit forms in "habit loops," which consist of three components: cue (or trigger), routine (the actual behavior or action), and reward. Initially, a cue, which can be an event or situation, triggers the brain to enter an automatic mode and select a habit to use. Following the cue is the routine, the actual behavior or action carried out in response. Completing the loop is the reward, a positive feedback that informs the brain whether this habit loop is worth retaining for future scenarios. Recognizing this cycle has profound implications for creating or modifying routines. For instance, if someone wants to develop a new morning exercise habit, they could set an alarm as the cue, do a brief workout as the routine, and then relish a tasty yet nutritious breakfast as the reward.

When there is a reward, there is an endorphin release and a feeling of accomplishment, known as "feel-good" chemicals. The chemical is naturally released after completing tasks, achieving goals, or even simply ticking off items from a to-do list, which can trigger a release of endorphins. The release of endorphins acts as a natural reward mechanism, reinforcing the behavior that led to the accomplishment. And, over time, as you associate routines with the positive feelings of accomplishment and the endorphin release, you become more motivated to maintain and adhere to your routine.

To ensure you have an effective and sustainable routine, consider key elements for a solid routine. Firstly, consistency is about maintaining a regular pattern, ensuring tasks are performed similarly over extended periods. This regularity not only reinforces habits but also fosters discipline and reduces the mental effort of decision-making. For example, if you aim to nurture a reading habit, consistently reading every night at 9 p.m. can be helpful.

Secondly, routines must possess flexibility—the capacity to adapt based on changing situations or needs. This adaptability ensures routines remain relevant, catering to unforeseen life events or changes. Take a workout routine, for instance; if an injury occurs, it's beneficial to transition from running to a less strenuous activity like swimming.

The third component, balance, emphasizes allotting adequate time to various life areas, such as work, relaxation, and self-improvement. This balanced approach not only wards off feelings of burnout but also guarantees holistic well-being. An effective way to achieve this might be designing a weekly routine that equally prioritizes work, relaxation, hobbies, and continuous learning.

The fourth element is specificity, which is about tailoring a routine to fit your goals. By crafting your routine around your goal, you ensure clarity, direction, and the elimination of unproductive tasks. For instance, if becoming an entrepreneur is the goal, then learning how to maintain a profit & loss statement will be pivotal.

Lastly, simplicity champions the idea of starting with basic routines and progressively enhancing them. This incremental approach reduces initial overwhelm, ensuring smoother adoption and mastery. If meditation is a sought-after habit, starting with a daily 5-minute session before increasing the duration is a practical approach.

In essence, integrating these foundational elements—consistency, flexibility, balance, specificity, and simplicity—into your routine enhances your long-term effectiveness and ensures you remain aligned with your evolving goals and lifestyles.

Don't just wing life; you should really consider a solid routine. I would even challenge you to create a 7-day routine; do the same thing every day. Try out your routine for 2-3 consecutive days at least, and challenge yourself until you can commit to the routine for seven days straight. It sounds impossible, but just try it.

Use the space below to start laying out a routine for yourself. There is an undated daily page in the Daily Execution Planner for you to write down your routine for the day and organize each day. Let's start by writing out your ideal routine for the next seven days below.

Sunday:

_____
_____
_____
_____
_____
_____
_____
_____
_____
_____
_____
_____
_____
_____
_____
_____

Monday:

_____
_____
_____
_____
_____
_____
_____
_____
_____
_____
_____
_____
_____
_____
_____

Tuesday:

_____

_____

_____

_____

_____

_____

_____

_____

_____

_____

_____

_____

_____

_____

Wednesday:

_____

_____

_____

_____

_____

_____

_____

_____

_____

_____

_____

_____

_____

_____

Thursday:

_____
_____
_____
_____
_____
_____
_____
_____
_____
_____
_____
_____
_____
_____
_____
_____
_____

Friday:

_____
_____
_____
_____
_____
_____
_____
_____
_____
_____
_____
_____
_____
_____
_____

Saturday:

_____
_____
_____
_____
_____
_____
_____
_____
_____
_____
_____
_____
_____
_____

Chapter 11

Assessing Progress Towards Your Goal

As you pursue your goals, regularly evaluating your progress is crucial. By doing so, you can determine if adjustments are necessary, be it in your daily routine or in setting achievable daily tasks. This not only allows you to gauge your trajectory but also helps you understand your emotions and assess if you're on the right path. Moreover, this self-assessment highlights what's effectively driving you closer to your goals and identifies methods to ensure consistent advancement.

Many successful and ambitious individuals attribute their achievements to this habit of introspection. I've personally found that when I take the time to reflect, I make vital adjustments that further deepen my self-awareness, helping me discern what strategies work best. This self-reflection has become an invaluable tool in enhancing my performance.

In the "Daily Execution Planner," I've intentionally incorporated moments for reflection at the close of each day and week. This design choice emphasizes the importance of documenting and evaluating daily activities to pinpoint what genuinely boosts your productivity. Every week, there are four pivotal questions to guide your introspection. The foremost among them invites you to celebrate your achievements. It prompts: "My most significant accomplishment of the week was..." This question encourages you to deliberate on your weekly highlights and identify moments that instilled a sense of pride.

In the planner, the subsequent prompt reads, "I was most proud of myself when..." This encourages introspection about those instances during the week when you paused, perhaps astounded by your own accomplishments, or felt a profound sigh of relief.

Another reflective statement to ponder over is, "My greatest lesson of the week was..." This isn't just about pinpointing mistakes but recognizing the learnings from them. Such moments might unveil surprising insights or those "aha!" realizations. It's worthwhile to document these since they might later be integrated into your Standard Operating Procedures (SOP). When recounting your journey or guiding someone else, these personal revelations will likely be the wisdom you impart.

Lastly, there's a contemplative statement, "If I could make one major adjustment leading into next week, I would..." This serves as an avenue for proactive thinking, focusing on continuous improvement. After all, the objective is consistent, incremental progress. Yet, achieving this requires assessing what might need a tweak, a fresh approach, or even a complete shift in your habits or routines to pave the way for the desired outcomes.

Let's take a moment and pause for you to reflect on each question. I would recommend trying this technique on Saturdays or Sundays.

My greatest accomplishment of the week was:

_____
_____
_____
_____
_____
_____
_____
_____
_____
_____
_____
_____
_____
_____
_____
_____
_____
_____
_____
_____
_____
_____
_____

I was most proud of myself when:

_____

_____

_____

_____

_____

_____

_____

_____

_____

_____

_____

_____

_____

_____

My greatest lesson of the week was:

_____

_____

_____

_____

_____

_____

_____

_____

_____

_____

_____

_____

If I could make one major improvement leading into next week I would:

_____

_____

_____

_____

_____

_____

_____

_____

_____

_____

_____

_____

Daily reflection holds as much significance as weekly introspection. Reflecting each day allows you to gauge your progress toward your goals, celebrate your achievements, and pinpoint areas that require more attention. This practice offers profound insights into your emotions, thoughts, and behaviors.

Reflection acts as a therapeutic conduit, aiding in the processing of day-to-day experiences and alleviating feelings of stress and anxiety. Engaging in new endeavors inevitably comes with its set of challenges. Without dedicated moments of reflection, emotions can accumulate, clouding your judgment and decision-making abilities. Regularly taking time to mentally unpack and process helps clear the mind, ensuring it stays sharp and focused.

Begin your daily reflections by asking, "What was my most significant achievement today?" This prompts you to identify and celebrate your main success of the day, offering a moment of self-recognition and affirmation.

Next, pose the question, "What worked well for me today?" Reflect on the steps you took that advanced you towards your goals, evaluate which aspects of your routine proved beneficial, and contemplate the moments of the day that brought you joy.

Then, ponder the question, "What didn't work well for me today?" This prompts you to identify areas for enhancement and reflect on potential improvements. Such introspection heightens your self-awareness, and it's precisely in these moments that personal growth is cultivated.

Lastly, ask yourself, "What will I improve for tomorrow?" This encourages you to identify a concrete step you can implement immediately the following day. By consistently reflecting and acting on this insight, you'll undoubtedly witness steady progress that drives you closer to your goals.

The Daily Execution Planner is designed with daily prompts to assist you in reflecting upon and recording your progress. These tools are invaluable for evaluating your journey toward your goals and making consistent improvements. I highly recommend exploring both the weekly reflection section and the daily insights in the planner. By incorporating these, you'll be on a path of steady and impactful progress.

Let's take time to complete a daily reflection now to see if it helps you.

What was my most significant achievement today?

_____
_____
_____
_____
_____
_____
_____
_____
_____
_____

What worked well for me today?

_____
_____
_____
_____
_____
_____
_____
_____
_____
_____

What didn't work well for me today?

_____
_____
_____
_____
_____
_____
_____
_____
_____
_____
_____
_____
_____
_____

What will I improve for tomorrow?

_____
_____
_____
_____
_____
_____
_____
_____
_____
_____
_____

Reflecting doesn't need to be time-consuming. Typically, 10-15 minutes can be sufficient. However, the value you derive depends on the effort you invest. Engaging deeply with these exercises can be transformative, fueling your personal growth. By embracing this process, you're setting yourself up to undoubtedly achieve your goals.

I highly urge you to maintain a journal too, chronicling every step of your journey. Venturing into uncharted territory, as you are now, paves the way for others to follow in your footsteps. Inevitably, many will inquire, 'How did you achieve that? Can you guide me?' Having a detailed account not only helps you show them the way but also serves as a reference should you need to retrace your steps. Think of this as creating your own Standard Operating Procedures (SOP), a term familiar in the corporate world.

By documenting, you equip yourself with a roadmap to review and refine. It becomes invaluable when, years down the line, you wonder, 'How did I accomplish that?' Your well-documented journey can provide answers and ensure neither you nor anyone else repeats the same mistakes.

As you advance on this path, a deep transformation awaits you. You'll become braver, more daring, and rise to levels you once thought were out of reach simply because you had the courage to embrace the unknown. It reminds me of a Jay-Z lyric: "People look at you strangely, saying you changed like you worked that hard to stay the same." So true!

Congratulations on completing "Goal Crusher"! You're now primed to achieve your big, audacious goals. Reaching this stage signals your deep understanding of what's required to seize your aspirations.

Always remember, it's the consistent, incremental actions that make the difference. Each step, no matter how small, moves you closer to your desired outcome. The emphasis is on embracing the process and the routines you've established. Commit to them, trust in them. Your journey as a Goal Crusher won't always be smooth. Moments of doubt and hesitation are inevitable. Life will test you to see how badly you really want it. It's all a part of the process. When faced with the urge to surrender, persevere because it's a sign that you're nearing your goal. Trust in yourself and the vision you've set. But don't give up!

In my own journey, I sought strength and direction through prayer. I also empowered myself with daily affirmations, believing in the power of my words. Whenever negativity threatened, I would counter it with gratitude and positive reflection. And there was nothing like calling my best friends for a little encouragement along the way.

This journey is transformative. Embrace the person that you'll become. You will be so proud of yourself and what you've achieved because you stayed committed to the process. Celebrate every single milestone, no matter how minor or major. It's these moments of recognition that fuel your dedication and drive.

Consistently immerse yourself in your goal. If you're eyeing your first investment property, explore similar properties or make a habit of attending Open Houses. Surround yourself with the ambiance of your aspirations. I recall when I aimed to join a Big Four firm, I'd sit in the office lobby, watching employees and visualizing myself as one of them. And when I got my offer letter, it was EVERYTHING! Before my acceptance to Emory's Goizueta Business School, I'd studied for the GMAT at their library, feeling the essence of being an Emory student.

Coco Gauff's victory at the US Open serves as a testament to visiting your goal often. After watching Serena Williams play at the US Open as a young girl, Coco went on to clinch the title herself, becoming the youngest to do so since Serena's own victory. She credited her win to her parents, exposing her to the game of tennis and creating experiences to help her believe that she could become a world-renowned professional tennis player. This encapsulates the essence of living your dream before its realization.

Embrace the journey with its highs and lows, knowing that it will culminate in unparalleled satisfaction. With the tools and strategies this book has equipped you with, I am confident in your success. Here's to your future triumphs! I have faith in you; you're destined for greatness. Congratulations in advance! You got this, Goal Crusher!

If you want more tools and information, follow me at **@iam_aprilsmith** on IG. Visit my website at **www.theoneday.co** to purchase your very own Daily Execution Planner.

Let's Crush It!

www.ingramcontent.com/pod-product-compliance
Lightning Source LLC
LaVergne TN
LVHW011336080426
835513LV00006B/381